WITH
COURAGE

SEVEN WOMEN
WHO CHANGED
AMERICA

BY LYNEA BOWDISH

MONDO

For Adelaide Attard, Former Commissioner, Nassau County,
New York, Department of Senior Citizen Affairs:
A woman of courage and dignity – L.B.

TEXT COPYRIGHT © 2004 by Lynea Bowdish

PHOTOGRAPH CREDITS

Cover, pp. 6, 27: © Bettman/CORBIS; cover, p. 12: © 1980, The Washington Post. Photo by Ken Haller. Reprinted with permission; cover, p. 18: © Angela Torres Los Angeles Photographer; cover, pp. 24, 29: © Charlie L. Soap; cover, p. 30: © Cheung Ching-Ming; cover, p. 36: Courtesy of the McGrath family; cover, p. 42: © Tina Hager/White House; p. 8: © Underwood & Underwood/CORBIS; pp. 9, 26: © corbisstockmarket.com; p. 10: © Digital Vision/Getty Images; p. 11: © Erich Hartmann/Magnum Photos; p. 14: © Courtesy of the Estate of Katharine Graham; p. 15: © AP/Wide World Photos; p. 16: © Royalty-Free/CORBIS; p. 17: © AFP/CORBIS; p. 20 (top): © James Leynse/CORBIS SABA; p. 20 (bottom): © Peter Turnley/CORBIS; p. 21: © Danny Lehman/CORBIS; p. 22: © Ted Streshinsky/CORBIS; p. 28: Original painting by Guy C. Reid, from "Seal of the Cherokee Nation" by Muriel H. Wright. The Chronicles of Oklahoma, Vol. XXXIV, Summer 1956; p. 32: © James P. Blair/CORBIS; p. 33: © Brand X/Roberstock.com; p. 34: © Izzy Schwartz/Photodisc Green/Getty Images; p. 38: From the Department of the Navy [Disclaimer: Neither the Department of the Navy nor any other component of the Department of Defense has approved, endorsed, or authorized this book]; p. 39: © Craig Rothhammer, National Association of Fleet Tug Sailors; p. 40: © CORBIS; p. 44: © University of Denver, Penrose Library Special Collections; p. 45: © CORBIS SYGMA; p. 46: © Photodisc Collection/Photodisc Blue/Getty Images

FOR INFORMATION CONTACT:

MONDO Publishing
980 Avenue of the Americas
New York, NY 10018

Visit our web site at http://www.mondopub.com

Printed in China

04 05 06 07 08 09   9 8 7 6 5 4 3 2 1

ISBN 1-59336-280-3

EDITED BY Susan DerKazarian
DESIGNED BY Michelle Farinella

Library of Congress Cataloging-in-Publication Data

Bowdish, Lynea.
  With courage : seven women who changed America / by Lynea Bowdish.
    p. cm.
  Includes index.
  Summary: Profiles seven American women--Rachel Carson, Katharine Graham, Dolores Huerta, Wilma Mankiller, Maya Lin, Kathleen McGrath, and Condoleezza Rice--who came to prominence within the last fifty years, focusing on each one's achievements and role as a pioneer.
    ISBN 1-59336-280-3 (pbk.)
    1. Women--United States--Biography--Juvenile literature. 2. Women in public life--United States--Biography--Juvenile literature. 3. Women civic leaders--United States--Biography--Juvenile literature. [1. Women--biography. 2. Women in public life.] I. Title.

HQ1412.B66 2004

2003059347

CONTENTS

INTRODUCTION

YOU ARE ABOUT TO MEET

SEVEN AMAZING WOMEN.

At first you might think these women have nothing in common. Their economic backgrounds are different. They are from different ethnic groups. Their achievements are in different areas, too—environmental science, publishing, social action, art and architecture, the military, and politics.

You might wonder why they're all included in the same book.

It turns out they are alike in some important ways.

The first thing these seven women have in common is that each is an American. The next link is that each of these women became well-known during the last fifty years or so. What else do they have in common? Look deeper. As you read, you may notice that each woman had a desire to learn more about the world.

That's enough right there to explain why these seven women are included in the same book. But wait. There's more. Each of these women was also a pioneer. They didn't set out to change their world . . . but that's what happened.

As they followed their dreams, worked, and studied, they found themselves moving into areas that were dominated by men. This made things difficult for each and every one of them. They met resistance from many people, including those they worked with and others working in their fields. Despite this resistance, they kept going. This, of course, took courage.

Each of these women had the courage to go beyond the limits that society had set for her. They had the courage to believe in themselves and their abilities. This courage, perhaps more than anything else, is the link that draws these women together. Because of their courage, they each had a part in changing America.

Rachel Carson

SAVING THE SPRING

DO YOU LIKE SPRINGTIME? Maybe you like listening to the birds chirp in the morning or to the frogs croak in the evening. But what if spring arrived one day and it was silent?

Rachel Carson warned that this could happen. She saw how chemicals being used were affecting the environment. She said if we kept using them, birds, insects, and other animals could disappear forever. Rachel spoke out for nature and all living things. Fortunately, people listened to her.

Rachel Carson was born on a farm in Pennsylvania in 1907. As a child, she knew she wanted to be a writer. Her first story was published in a magazine for children when she was only ten years old!

Rachel also loved nature. Her mother encouraged Rachel's love of writing and the outdoors. But Rachel never imagined that when she grew up she would be able to combine the two.

When Rachel was eighteen years old, she went to Pennsylvania College for Women. There, she discovered science. Back then, women usually didn't study science. But Rachel did. She studied biology, the

Rachel Carson looking through a microscope

science of living things.

Rachel graduated in 1929. That summer, she worked at a marine laboratory in Woods Hole, Massachusetts. Rachel fell in love with the ocean and all the wonderful things living in it.

But Rachel didn't just stay in the laboratory. She waded in tidal pools and studied the life she found there. Years later, she even went deep-sea diving. Rachel did many things women back then usually didn't do.

In 1935, Rachel went to work for the U.S. Bureau of Fisheries. Here, both her science and writing skills were important. Her job was to write radio programs. She explained science in a way that the people listening could understand, even if they didn't know anything about science. She worked hard and became the editor-in-chief of publications at the U.S. Fish and Wildlife Service.

Rachel's home life wasn't easy during these years. In 1935, her father died, and she helped support her mother. Soon after, her sister died, and her sister's two daughters came to live with Rachel and her mother.

But Rachel continued her scientific studies and her writing. She wrote a book about the sea called *Under the Sea-Wind*. The book was published in 1941. But because World War II had just started, the book didn't sell well.

Ten years later, in 1951, Rachel's second book was published. In it,

Rachel explained the science of the ocean in ways everyone could understand. *The Sea Around Us* was a big success. A year later, Rachel left the Fish and Wildlife Service so she could write full-time.

For years, Rachel had been interested in pesticides. Pesticides are chemicals that are used to kill the insects and other small animals that eat and harm crops grown on farms. Chemical companies and the U.S. Department of Agriculture were promoting their use in order to protect crops.

pesticides being sprayed

But Rachel was concerned about pesticides, especially one called DDT. She wondered if they could be harmful to fish, animals, and crops. . . and people, too. She began studying what scientists were finding out about pesticides. Then she decided to write about it.

It took Rachel a long time to write the book *Silent Spring.* Things kept happening in her life that made it difficult to find the time to write. She was often sick. Her niece died in 1957, and Rachel adopted and took care of her niece's young son. Then, in 1958, Rachel's mother died. But Rachel believed so strongly in what she had to say about the dangers of pesticides that she finished the book despite these difficulties.

Silent Spring was published in 1962. In it, Rachel warned that pesticides were harmful to all parts of the environment. She warned that there might come a time when spring would, indeed, be silent. And because Rachel believed that everything in nature was related, she warned that pesticides could hurt people, too.

How can pesticides hurt people as well as plants and animals? It has to do with what biologists call the food chain. When a pesticide is added to the soil to kill the insects and other animals eating and damaging crops, it can affect the crops, too. When people or animals eat these treated crops, they can get sick or die from the pesticide. Rain also washes pesticides into rivers and streams, affecting the plants and fish in the water. Anything that then eats those plants or animals also eats the pesticide.

These fish died after the river they lived in was polluted with chemicals.

As Rachel says in *Silent Spring*, you don't have to spray pesticides directly on a robin to kill it. If you spray a tree to kill a pest, the pest dies, and everything seems okay. In autumn, the leaf falls, and time passes. An earthworm eats the leaf, and later, a robin eats the worm. The pesticide gets into the bird's body and there's a good chance it will die. This food chain exists all through nature. People are part of it, too, absorbing pesticides that are in the plants or animals they eat.

Rachel's book angered the chemical industry and the Department of Agriculture. They said that Rachel was wrong about pesticides. After all, what did a woman know about science?

But Rachel was brave. She stood her ground and insisted she was right. Rachel was well-known as a scientist. Her readers could understand what she was saying and they listened to her.

The government started looking carefully at pesticides. Rachel appeared before a Congressional Committee that was interested in the possible effects of pesticides. She explained to this group of leaders what was happening to our natural world. She suggested that the government adopt policies to protect the environment from further damage by pesticides.

Rachel helped people understand that everything in nature is related. She also helped people realize that we are responsible for taking care of the world around us.

Rachel Carson died of cancer in 1964 at the age of fifty-six. But her bravery and dedication live on in the environmental movement.

There is still much to do. Although the use of DDT was banned, other pesticides are still used. Undoing the harm done to nature takes a long time. Because of Rachel, we are now aware of our effect on nature. Hopefully, we will continue to learn how to make our impact on nature less harmful and more helpful.

FOR AS RACHEL BELIEVED, BY HELPING NATURE, WE ARE HELPING OURSELVES.

Katharine Graham

FACING NEW CHALLENGES

WHEN KATHARINE GRAHAM'S husband died in 1963, she didn't have to find work to support herself and her children. She and her family were wealthy. Despite this, she chose to take over her husband's job at the *Washington Post*, a newspaper in Washington, D.C. This was a choice that would affect more than just the *Washington Post* or Katharine's life—it would affect the whole world.

Katharine Meyer (her last name became Graham when she married) was born in New York in 1917. Her father was a banker and her mother was a writer. Most people would have said that Katharine was a lucky child. Her family was wealthy. They had several homes, and they traveled. To an outsider, Katharine's life probably seemed perfect.

But it was also a lonely life. Both of her parents were away much of the time. Katharine went to an all-girls boarding school, a school where she and the other students lived. She only went home once in a while. Katharine also went away to college. There, she studied journalism, which taught her how to write for newspapers.

Katharine graduated in 1938. By that time, her father had bought

*Katharine Meyer, at about
eight years old*

a Washington, D.C., newspaper named the *Washington Post*. Katharine began working for the paper (which was called the *Post* for short).

Katharine's life soon changed again. She met Phil Graham, a young lawyer. They were married in 1940, and Katharine quit her job and became a housewife and mother. Her most important role in life became taking care of her family. With four children to raise, she kept busy.

Then Katharine's father made her husband, Phil, publisher of the *Post*. It wasn't surprising that Phil got the job instead of Katharine. Back then, women usually didn't have important jobs in business or journalism. Katharine herself didn't seem to question her father's decision at all.

In 1963, Katharine's life changed once more. Phil died. People thought Katharine would sell the *Washington Post*. But Katharine wanted to keep the newspaper for her children. So, at the age of forty-six, she took on a huge challenge. She took over the *Washington Post* herself.

Katharine was shy, quiet, and unsure of herself. She was one of only a few women in the man's world of the newspaper business. But Katharine was also smart. She was interested in what was going on around her. She also had some journalism experience. So Katharine asked questions and learned quickly.

In 1975, Katharine Graham (front left) was the only woman heading up a major newspaper in America.

Katharine knew that some of the men weren't happy that she was in charge. But Katharine kept learning. She began to make decisions about the direction she wanted the *Post* to take. That direction included telling the truth through the newspaper.

In 1971, *The New York Times*, a newspaper in New York City, began publishing government papers about the Vietnam War. These became known as the Pentagon Papers. They showed that the government had not been telling the truth about the Vietnam War. The government had been hiding many of its activities.

Since the beginning of the Vietnam War, many Americans had wondered if the country should have become involved. In 1971, some people were still against the war. And if the Pentagon Papers became public, even more people would probably turn against the war.

The government tried to stop the publication of the Pentagon

Papers. Then Katharine stepped in. She wanted the *Post* to be part of letting the public know the truth.

Watergate building, Washington, D.C.

The publishing of the Pentagon Papers had several effects. Even more Americans came to realize we should no longer be involved in the Vietnam War. More people started calling for peace. Eventually, the war ended.

By publishing the Pentagon Papers, it's possible that Katharine and the *Post* shortened the length of the war. Publishing the papers also moved the *Washington Post* into the spotlight. No longer was it just a local newspaper. It had became an important national newspaper.

The following year, in 1972, Katharine supported her staff in publishing the story of the Watergate scandal. President Richard Nixon was running for reelection. He was a Republican. Men working to get him reelected had broken into the Democratic Party headquarters. They wanted to find out what the Democrats were planning. If they knew this information, they might be able to help President Nixon win the election. The headquarters were at the Watergate building in Washington, D.C., so this became known as the Watergate scandal.

Under Katharine's orders, journalists at the *Washington Post* investigated the scandal and the crimes that had been committed. They did this by finding out the details and then supporting those details with solid factual information.

The scandal and the crimes turned out to be far more than a few men acting on their own. President Nixon and his staff had ordered the break-in. When their involvement was discovered, Richard Nixon resigned from the presidency.

After this national crisis, Katharine continued building up the *Post*, making it even better and more important. She faced other problems, such as a strike by some newspaper workers. But she got through them and kept the *Post* in business.

In 1974, U.S. President Richard Nixon announced his resignation after the Watergate scandal.

Katharine stepped down as publisher in 1979. But she never stopped being involved with the *Post*. The newspaper was important to her.

In 1997, at the age of eighty-four, Katharine took on another new challenge. She wrote her first book. It was a book about her life and was called *Personal History*. In 1998, the book won the Pulitzer Prize, a prize given for excellence in writing.

Katharine died in 2001. She lived a remarkable life. She was never too old to be interested in the world or to take on new challenges.

IT WAS BY FACING THESE CHALLENGES THAT KATHARINE GRAHAM HAD A PART IN CHANGING THE WORLD FOR THE BETTER.

Dolores Huerta

MAKING IT HAPPEN

SÍ, SE PUEDE [SEE, say PWAY-day]. This is Spanish for "yes, it can be done." It is a motto of the United Farm Workers Union. And it is Dolores Huerta [WHERE-tuh] who gets things done; she helps farmworkers get what they need to lead better lives.

Dolores, who is Mexican American, was born in 1930 in the state of New Mexico. When her parents divorced, she and her mother and two brothers moved to California.

Dolores's mother ran a hotel where many farmworkers stayed. It wasn't a fancy hotel, but sometimes the workers could barely pay for their rooms. Dolores began to realize that the farmworkers needed help.

Why did they need help? Because these poor workers had no one to speak up for them. The workers came from Mexico and other countries, and they often could not speak English well. They worked for whatever money they were offered.

They worked mainly for fruit and vegetable growers in California and other parts of the United States. Dolores knew they were paid little. She knew they often slept in run-down shacks with no running water or indoor toilets.

These people are called migrant workers. When one crop is picked, the migrant workers move on to another farm to pick another crop— and so on, farm after farm. It's hard work, picking crops in the fields under the hot sun. Often, the children of the workers must also work so the families can earn enough money to eat.

A Mexican migrant worker must share this small, dirty kitchen with many others.

A young migrant worker picks strawberries in a field in California.

As Dolores was growing up, she saw how hard the lives of these workers were. She wanted to do something for them. Dolores's mother had taught her that helping people was a good thing.

Dolores went to college and became a teacher. As a teacher, she saw migrant workers' children coming to school hungry and wearing shoes with holes in them. Dolores was already helping by teaching these children how to speak, read, and write in English. But she wanted to do more. So she left teaching and began working for a community group that helped people lead better lives.

As part of her job, Dolores worked as a lobbyist. A lobbyist is someone who talks to the people who pass laws. The lobbyist tries to convince them to pass laws that will help certain groups of people. Dolores tried to get lawmakers to pass laws that would help the migrant workers.

A migrant worker unloads a bushel of red peppers in California.

In the 1950s and 1960s, it was unusual for a woman to be a lobbyist. But Dolores did it anyway. It was while she was lobbying for workers' rights that Dolores met Cesar Chavez [SAY-sar SHAV-ez]. Cesar also wanted to help migrant workers. So Dolores and Cesar left their jobs and, in 1962, formed what would later become the United Farm Workers Union (UFW).

Things weren't easy for Dolores. By then, she had her own children to support. And, like being a lobbyist, forming and leading unions wasn't something women did in the 1960s. But Dolores did it anyway.

The work was hard. Dolores was away from home a lot, trying to convince workers to join the union. Many workers were afraid of the growers for whom they worked. The workers thought the growers would be angry if they joined the union. And they had little money to pay union dues, the money it cost to join. But Dolores was able to convince many

Cesar Chavez speaks at a labor union rally in California in 1966.

workers to join the union. By joining, they were supporting La Causa [LA COW-zuh], "The Cause" of the migrant workers. The union grew.

Then the UFW called for a huelga [WHEL-guh], a strike against the growers. The migrant workers would refuse to work until the growers agreed to pay them better wages. But in order to get support from the public, the UFW needed to make people understand why they were striking. To do this, Dolores organized picket lines in front of the farms. People on picket lines walked back and forth carrying signs to support La Causa.

Dolores's work was dangerous. The UFW did not use violence to get the growers to listen to them, but the growers still became angry. Fights broke out. Dolores was threatened by people who didn't believe the workers should be helped. She thought she might be hurt at any time.

Then the UFW called for a boycott of grapes. The boycott meant that people wouldn't buy grapes until the growers listened to the union. The boycott spread from California to other parts of the United States.

Finally, some of the growers began dealing with the union. They signed agreements with the union that gave the workers higher pay and some benefits. Dolores wrote the agreements between the union and the growers. That, too, was unusual for a woman to do. But Dolores did it anyway. The grape boycott ended.

Not all the growers agreed to the changes, however. And so the struggle went on. The union became part of a bigger, more powerful union called the AFL-CIO.

Cesar Chavez died in 1993, but Dolores continues working for La Causa. She knows that sí, se puede. . .yes, it can be done.

Dolores's family is large now. She has eleven children, fourteen grandchildren, and even some great-grandchildren. They support her efforts to help the migrant workers.

The hard times for these workers haven't ended, though. Many growers still won't deal with the union. They don't want to pay workers fair wages, or provide benefits. But Dolores believes in La Causa and in the idea that she can help make the lives of migrant workers better.

Dolores has received many awards for her work. More than forty years after taking up this cause, she still continues to struggle for the rights of farmworkers.

AND WITH DOLORES WORKING AT THIS,
SÍ, SE PUEDE.

Wilma Mankiller

FINDING THE WAY HOME

IN 1969, A GROUP OF Native Americans took over Alcatraz Island off the coast of San Francisco in California. This island was the site of a former prison. The Native Americans wanted to call attention to the many problems they had in this country. The problems had been going on for hundreds of years, ever since the first Europeans came to and settled in North America. The new settlers saw the native people as wild and dirty. Because the new settlers thought they were better than the Native Americans, they treated them badly. This is called discrimination and it went on for years and years.

By the 1960s, many Native Americans could not find jobs or decent housing because of discrimination. They had few opportunities for good health care and education, and as a result, many Native Americans were poor. The protest at Alcatraz was an attempt to change some of this.

Wilma Mankiller saw what was happening at Alcatraz. She was a Cherokee. The Cherokee are one of many different groups of Native American people. She was living in San Francisco with her husband and two daughters at the time. Wilma began to help raise money for the

Alcatraz Island, in the San Francisco Bay

protest against the problems faced by Native Americans.

The Alcatraz protest changed things for Wilma. It opened her eyes to the Native Americans' problems, and it would eventually lead to her becoming the principal chief of the Cherokee Nation. She would be the first woman to hold that office.

Wilma Pearl Mankiller was born in Oklahoma in 1945. Her father was Cherokee. Her mother was not Native American—she was part Dutch and part Irish. In Cherokee history, "Mankiller" was an honored title given to someone who protected the Cherokee village. One of Wilma's ancestors had taken on this title, and it became the family name.

Wilma grew up on a farm with her ten brothers and sisters. The house had no electricity or running water. But there was a lot to do on the farm, and Wilma was happy there.

Then their land began drying up. It hardly rained for two years. There was no way for the Mankillers to make a living. So Wilma and her family moved. The Bureau of Indian Affairs, part of the U.S. government, thought Native Americans would be able to find jobs and houses more easily in the cities. So they moved these families off their farms and into the cities.

Wilma and her family moved to San Francisco. Everything was different in the city—the noise, the large numbers of people, the tall buildings. But there was something even worse. Wilma and her family were far away from their friends and from their land in Oklahoma.

But after a while, Wilma got used to her new life. She went to school and then to college. She got married and had two children. Then Wilma learned about the people on Alcatraz Island who were protesting the Native Americans' problems. Since Wilma was a Cherokee, they were her problems, too.

Native Americans took over Alcatraz Island as a protest against their problems.

Wilma helped raise money for the protesters. But Wilma knew she could do more to help. And to do more, she knew she had to return to Oklahoma and to her Cherokee people. Wilma and her husband separated, and in 1976 Wilma and her daughters went home to

Oklahoma. They moved near Tahlequah, the capital of the Cherokee Nation.

Wilma started writing letters and filling out forms to get government money for Cherokee programs. She helped in other ways, too. She saw that the Cherokees needed running water and better homes. So Wilma helped put in water systems. She also worked to build and repair people's houses.

There was still more for Wilma to do. It was time for her to help lead the Cherokee Nation. In 1985, Wilma became principal chief.

When Wilma ran for office, there were protests from the Cherokee. Many years before, Cherokee women had been important in the running of the tribe. They helped make decisions. Some women were given the title "Beloved Woman," which meant their advice was valued. But things changed after European settlers came to North America. Some of the Cherokee had begun to believe a woman shouldn't be chief.

But Wilma won anyway. Wilma was the first woman to be elected principal chief of the Cherokee Nation. The position was like running a small country.

Wilma had many health problems throughout these years. After a car accident, she spent months in the hospital. Then she found out she had a disease that affects the muscles and makes them weak. Later still, Wilma had to have a kidney transplant.

In spite of all this, Wilma kept working for the Cherokee people. She encouraged them to help their community. And she made non-Native Americans in the United States aware of Cherokee problems.

Wilma remarried in 1986. Her husband, Charlie Soap, is a Cherokee who knows the Cherokee language. Wilma feels that young Cherokees should learn about the culture and language of their people. So she helped set up a summer program where Cherokees can learn their own language. But Wilma's health wasn't good. When it came time for reelection in 1995, she decided not to run.

Wilma found her way back home to the land of her ancestors, to the land of the Cherokee. By doing so, she was able to help her people and continues to help them today. Wilma will always be known as the first woman to be principal chief of the Cherokee.

BUT EVEN MORE IMPORTANT, SHE WILL BE KNOWN FOR HELPING NATIVE AMERICANS LIVE BETTER LIVES.

Maya Lin

HEALING A NATION

BY THE TIME MAYA LIN was twenty-one years old, she was famous. No, she wasn't an Olympic athlete, a movie actress, or even a rock star. She was an architect and sculptor. An architect is someone who plans how buildings are to be built. A sculptor makes figures or statues. And architects and sculptors don't usually become famous by the age of twenty-one.

Maya didn't set out to be famous. She just entered a contest. The contest was to design a memorial to honor those who had served in the Vietnam War.

Maya won the contest. That's when the trouble started. Maya's design was different than people expected. It wasn't a statue of soldiers or battles or guns. It was a wall made of black stone. And on the wall were the names of all those who had died or were listed as missing in action in the Vietnam War.

Many people didn't like this idea for a memorial. They also didn't like that the design had been created by a college student who was so young, who was a woman, and who was Asian American.

Maya's parents were both from China. They came to the United

Vietnam War memorial, designed by Maya Lin

States in 1948 and settled in Ohio. They both got jobs teaching at Ohio University.

Maya was born in 1959. As she grew up, her parents encouraged her to decide for herself what she wanted to do. So when Maya went to Yale University in Connecticut, she decided to study architecture and sculpture.

Maya's teachers wanted her to focus on one subject. But Maya was interested in both, and so she studied both. Then, when she was in her last year of college, Maya heard about the contest. A group of people had collected money to build a memorial in Washington, D.C. The memorial would honor those who had served in the Vietnam War.

Many people in the United States had not supported the Vietnam War. During the years that it lasted, the war caused a lot of arguments and trouble in the nation. But a few years after it ended, people wanted to remember those who had served in the war.

Maya's design for the memorial was different than most memorials. The memorial is made of two walls of black stone. The two walls meet at an angle. Visitors to the memorial enter from either end using a pathway. They walk down a long sloping sidewalk. As they walk down the path, the wall gets taller. When they reach the bottom of the slope, the path goes up again in the other direction and the wall gets shorter until it ends at ground level.

More than 58,000 names—of Americans who died or went missing during the Vietnam War— are inscribed on The Wall.

On the wall are the names of those Americans who died or were listed as missing during the Vietnam War. Over 58,000 names are on the wall. The names are in the order in which the people died or went missing.

Some people protested the design. These people included veterans who had served in and survived the war, politicians, and others. But

*The Wall at night, with the Washington
Monument in the background*

"The Wall," as it came to be called, was built using Maya's design anyway.

There were compromises, however. Two traditional statues were added, as well as a United States flag. But none of these were placed close enough to The Wall to spoil its effect.

And The Wall's effect was powerful. It was dedicated in 1982, and people were drawn to it right away. They came to see the names. And because the black stone was polished, they could also see their own reflections in The Wall. They felt a part of those who had served and had been lost.

And for some reason, most visitors felt the need to touch The Wall.

And they remembered. Not the war, but the people who were lost in the war. Maya's design gave Americans a chance to mourn and remember the brave people who had served and were now gone. It helped them forget the anger and trouble that the war had caused in the United States.

Maya is no longer twenty-one, of course. She is married now and has two children. She continues to design buildings and sculptures that put people in harmony with the world around them.

Among her other works, Maya designed a memorial in Montgomery, Alabama, to the civil rights movement. This movement worked to ensure rights for all people, no matter what their race or color. Maya has also created and built statues and landscapes for universities, private companies, and for individuals as well.

Maya's work has won many awards and can be seen all over the country. But for many people, her lasting and most famous work is the Vietnam Memorial. And the greatest experience for these people is to visit the memorial.

The Vietnam Memorial is the most visited memorial in the United States. It has the power to make viewers feel strong emotions. People visit Washington, D.C., to see The Wall, and touch it, and remember.

Maya's memorial did much to help heal the suffering from a war that had caused anger and hatred in this country. Maya showed that a young Asian female artist had something to say about war.

SHE FOCUSED A NATION'S ATTENTION NOT ON THE WAR, BUT ON THE PEOPLE WHO SERVED. MAYA'S MEMORIAL HELPED A NATION TO HEAL.

Kathleen McGrath

SEEING THE WORLD

WHEN KATHLEEN MCGRATH was appointed commander of the *USS Jarrett* in 1998, she became the first American woman to command, or be in control of, a warship. Some said the U.S. Navy gave her this job only because she was a woman. For years, the Navy hadn't welcomed women. Now they wanted to show that they had changed.

But people who knew Kathleen McGrath knew she was made commander because she was the best person for the job. She had worked hard to get ahead in the Navy. And she had trained for a long time.

As a child, Kathleen didn't think much about the Navy. Born in Columbus, Ohio, in 1952, she grew up on military bases because her father was an Air Force pilot. One of these bases was on the island of Guam in the Pacific Ocean. Her father was stationed there during the Vietnam War.

When Kathleen got older, she went to college in California. After college she worked for the U.S. Forestry Service, but she couldn't find a job there that she really liked. After several years, Kathleen decided she wanted to do something different. Her father suggested she join the Air

Force and try flying. As an Air Force pilot himself, he thought she would like it.

Kathleen decided to look into it. She went to the Air Force recruiting office, which is where people go to get information on joining. When Kathleen got there, the recruiter was at lunch. But the Navy recruiter was nearby, so Kathleen talked to him instead.

The recruiter spoke to Kathleen about the Navy. She was told she would see the world if she joined, and she was promised adventure. So Kathleen joined the Navy.

Women had started joining the Navy in 1812 as nurses. Later, they began doing other jobs, too. But these were jobs that kept them on land. Many people didn't think women should work on ships and go into battle. But by the time Kathleen joined the Navy, women were demanding equal jobs. The Armed Forces, including the Navy, had to change.

There was another reason why the Navy needed to change. The Navy had more than 300 ships, but not enough men were joining to work on all of those ships. So the Navy began encouraging women to join.

In 1978, the Navy finally said that women would be allowed to work on ships. But they wouldn't be able to work on combat ships, the ships that might be in a battle. According to some people, war was "man's work," and women wouldn't be good in combat. But other people thought women shouldn't be allowed on ships at all, even ships not going into combat. They said that having women and men serve together was a bad idea. They believed women weren't strong enough to work on ships. Besides, ships weren't built for housing both men and women. There wasn't enough room for separate spaces.

*Kathleen's first command was a submarine
rescue ship called the* USS Recovery.

But things kept changing. In 1994, women were finally allowed to serve on combat ships.

When Kathleen joined the Navy, she had no intention of taking an office job. She had been promised adventure, and that's what she wanted. After going to officer training school, Kathleen went to sea, getting experience working on different kinds of ships.

Her travels on these ships took her around the world. She served in the Western Pacific, the Mediterranean, the Caribbean, and the Persian Gulf. In 1993, Kathleen was given her first command, the *USS Recovery*. This ship wasn't a warship, but it gave Kathleen experience being a commander.

In 1998, Kathleen became the first woman in charge of a warship when she was made commander of the USS Jarrett.

Then, in 1998, Kathleen was made commander of the USS *Jarrett*, a warship. Kathleen was the first American woman to be in charge of a warship. The ship was 453 feet [138 m] long, bigger than a football field. It carried 1,100-pound [499-kg] missiles. It also had a crew of 262 sailors. Of these 262, only four were women. And Kathleen was in charge.

Kathleen led the ship and crew to the Persian Gulf in the Middle East. Their job was to patrol the waters, looking for and stopping oil smugglers who were trying to illegally sell oil. The ship and its crew had spent more than a year training for their mission. It was a job with a lot of responsibility. . . and a lot of danger, as well.

It wasn't easy being away from home for so long. Kathleen was married, and she and her husband had adopted two young children from Russia. Like other Navy parents, Kathleen made videos of herself reading stories, which she would send home to her children. But, of course, they still missed each other.

After Kathleen became commander of the *USS Jarrett*, she was in the news a lot. People realized that this was an important step for all women. Women in the Navy were being treated equally in more and more situations. But Kathleen wasn't looking for attention. She focused on her job and did it well.

Kathleen served as commander for almost two years and was given the rank of captain in 2002. When Kathleen became ill with cancer, she retired from the Navy.

Kathleen died in 2002. She was fifty years old. Her family, of course, will remember her as a mother, wife, sister, and daughter. But for others, Kathleen will be remembered as the first woman commander of a U.S. warship. She did what many people thought a woman couldn't or shouldn't do. Kathleen led the way for other women who dream of commanding ships and having important careers in the Navy.

Through her work in the U.S. Navy, Captain Kathleen McGrath saw much of the world.

BUT SHE DID MORE THAN SEE THE WORLD — SHE ALSO HELPED CHANGE IT.

Condoleezza Rice

OVERCOMING THE ODDS

WHEN CONDOLEEZZA RICE was growing up, her parents told her she could be anything she wanted to be. They also told her that she'd have to be twice as good at it as everyone else.

Why? Because Condi, as she was known, was African American. And she was growing up in the South, in Birmingham, Alabama, during the 1950s and 1960s. The civil rights movement was exploding all around. The civil rights movement was an effort to end the segregation laws. The segregation laws meant that African Americans and Caucasians legally were separated from each other. African Americans couldn't go to the same schools as Caucasians. They couldn't eat in the same restaurants. And they had to ride in the backs of buses.

Many people wanted things to stay segregated. Others believed that all people should be treated equally. The disagreements resulted in protest marches and sometimes even bombings and other kinds of violent attacks.

But Condi's parents believed that education was the answer. They were sure that with study and hard work, Condi would become the

Condi went off to college at the University of Denver when she was just fifteen years old!

absolute best person she could be.

Condi was born on November 14, 1954. She and her family lived in a middle-class African American neighborhood. Both of Condi's parents were teachers. Her father was also a minister. Religion was a major part of her childhood. Another important part of Condi's childhood was music. The Rice family had always loved music. In fact, the name "Condoleezza" comes from an Italian musical term that means "with sweetness."

With the help of her grandmother and mother, Condi started playing the piano when she was three. But Condi's interests included other things, as well. She studied ballet, French, and ice-skating. And she read piles of books. Condi also learned to love football. She still does. Her father taught her about the game, and Condi became a big fan.

Condi was also interested in the subjects she learned at school. She was a quick learner. Condi's parents wanted her to be able to move at her own pace, so her mother taught her at home for a while. Because she studied at home and was intelligent and hardworking, Condi skipped two grades in elementary school. This meant she started college when she was fifteen.

Condoleezza Rice with President George W. Bush

At college, Condi turned away from her dreams of being a concert pianist. She decided to study the country that was then known as the Soviet Union. She even learned to speak Russian, one of the languages of the former Soviet Union. Condi began to spend more time studying foreign affairs, which is how countries deal with each other. But she never gave up the piano and still enjoys playing today.

After college, Condi began teaching at Stanford University in California. Later, she was named provost of the university. This meant that, among other things, she was in charge of the university's money and budget. It was an important job.

In 1999, Condi began an even more important job. George W. Bush, the governor of Texas, had decided to run for president of the United

White House, Washington, D.C.

States. Condi became his foreign affairs adviser during the campaign. Her job was to inform and advise George W. Bush about events going on in other countries.

Soon after George W. Bush was elected president in 2000, Condi became his national security adviser. The national security adviser gives the president advice on how to deal with other countries. For the first time in history, a woman holds this job. And for the first time, it is held by an African American. It is a job with great influence and power.

Once, when Condi was ten, she and her parents visited Washington, D.C. Like other tourists, they went to see the White House. Even though Condi hadn't been allowed to eat in some restaurants with Caucasian people, she still had dreams. On that day, Condi looked at the White

House and told her father that someday she was going to be inside that big, white house.

Condi achieved that goal. Today, she spends much of her time working in the White House with President George W. Bush and other leaders of our country.

Condi is blazing new trails in politics for women and African Americans. There is no doubt that her parents' advice and encouragement helped her become successful. And without her education, she couldn't have come so far. But it's Condi's personal qualities that make her what she is today. She was brought up to respect herself. She was brought up to believe she could do anything. She was taught to work hard.

Many people believe there's a lot more ahead for Condoleezza Rice. Some people even think that, in the future, she could become president of the United States of America.

No one knows for sure, of course. But if Condi does become president, she will have overcome the odds. She has already done what many people wouldn't imagine a young African American woman growing up in the segregated South could do—become the president's number one adviser.

NO MATTER WHAT CONDI ENDS UP DOING IN THE FUTURE, SHE WILL HAVE OVERCOME INCREDIBLE ODDS.

INDEX